Fragrance of Remembrance

THE BOOK OF BONITA

Bonita Blakeman

Fragrance of Remembrance - The Book of Bonita

Cover art by Steve Fryer
www.stevefryer.com

Book design and illustrations by Ruthann Fryer

Published by Seraph Creative 2025
United States / United Kingdom / South Africa / Australia
www.seraphcreative.org

Printed worldwide 2025

ISBN 978-1-964959-84-9 (paperback)

ISBN 978-1-964959-85-6 (eBook)

I dedicate this book to
Ruthann and Steve Fryer

Your love and work has made
this such a beautiful piece of art.
Words can't express my gratitude.
Thank you from the deepest
places of my heart.

I also dedicate this to the women of
The Sound of Paper.
You know who you are!

FOREWORD

Welcome to a fresh perspective of faith. You have entered the world of one of the most revolutionary and hopeful story tellers of our generation. This book comes filled with clarity, answers, and the motivation you have been searching for! These true stories were experienced in the midst of difficult and meaningful situations. The outcome of these experiences were simple yet they created profound SHIFTS in antiquated beliefs that no longer provided the support or answers that was needed. Just like Bonita - you and I have been asking for THE MORE and THE LORD has answered. In fact, we holding some of those answers in our hands right now! All we have to do is read!!!

Bonita's unusual insights and perspectives are life altering. Through her stories she offers unique opportunities to step beyond the limitations of what we already know- beyond the limitations of mainstream religious thought into the realm of ALL POSSIBILITIES! In every story there is a living stream of compassion with solid truth that opens the heart to hear without the noise of the past, the threats from fear of change, and the pressure to conform to an antiquated system. In this way Bonita is calling us all to come out from our religious hiding places. It's time to breathe again the Freedom that Messiah Yeshua granted us when He gave His life for us.

It is time for all of us to regain our power and live in His authority. So many beautiful Believers are yearning for this very thing.

In the past decade, I have personally experienced these profound liberating truths as I have had the privilege of walking with Bonita. Her generous servanthood and determined love for the LORD helped to reshape my faith and consequently my life.

By choosing to read this book you have made a profound investment in your own life and there will be fruit - lasting fruit for you and the LORD to enjoy for eternity.

It is one of my life's highest honors to recommend these writings from the heart of one of most loyal and dedicated Handmaidens of the LORD. Get ready for your SHIFT - to SEE with new eyes, FEEL with a new heart, and EXPERIENCE Yeshua as never before!

Dr. Yana Sanders

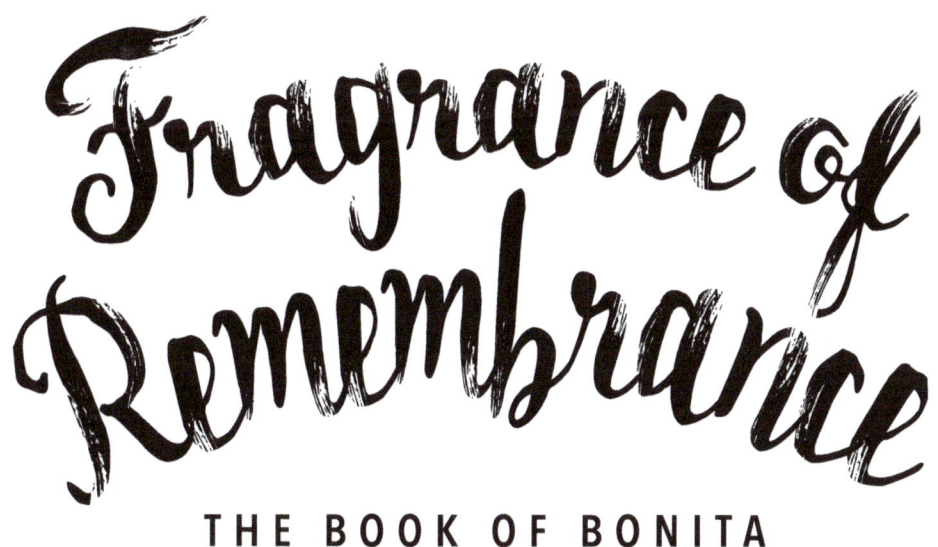

THE BOOK OF BONITA

Bonita Blakeman

Published by Seraph Creative

Table of Contents

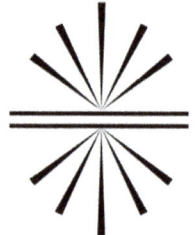

FRAGRANCE OF REMEMBRANCE

Book of Bonita

It's true—we all have a story to tell.

Not one etched in stone or carved with chisel and hammer, but written on the tender tablets of the heart. The kind Paul spoke of in 2 Corinthians 3—living letters, breathed into existence by the Spirit of God. Our stories are living words. Not just our history, but His-story—God walking with us, through us, in the messy and miraculous moments of life.

I've come to believe that our bodies, our hearts, our lived experiences—they matter deeply to heaven. He came in flesh, walked dusty roads, laughed, wept, bled, and rose. So how could He not care about our human journey?

Each of us carries a unique sound—an unseen melody vibrating in the fiber of our being. That's what this book is about. The fragrance of Jesus in my DNA. His story, sung through my life.

For a long time, I tried to tuck away the painful chapters. We all do. We try to forget or edit the hard parts. But even in the pain, He was there—writing redemption between the lines, bringing me from death to life. Again and again.

This is not just my story—it's our story. The testimony of the overcomers.

I remember, as a child, sitting in pews during testimony time. People would stand and tell what God was doing in their lives. And when someone really hit the mark—you could feel it. Like heaven cracked open for a moment, and we all got lifted. Encouraged. Fed.

Now, at 71, I understand more clearly the power of those moments. My life, like so many, has spoken. And now I feel it's time to write it down.

Like Habakkuk said: "Write the vision, make it plain so that all who pass by may read it."

If only you knew the fear I had about writing this! I almost didn't. I questioned if my story mattered, if I could find the words, if anyone would listen. But here I am. Brave enough, finally, to put pen to paper. To sing my song.

This book is the triumph of courage.

It's not a memoir of perfection. It's a tapestry. A collection of encounters, whispers, dreams, breakdowns, and breakthroughs. It's the overcomer's song in my key.

My hope? That as you read, something awakens in you.

That these stories light a fire in your heart—a passion to remember your own story, your own sound. That they call you back to the wonder of God in your everyday life. That they remind you that you're seen, deeply loved, and called to shine in ways only you can.

Let this book resurrect something inside you.

Let it stir you awake to the miraculous all around you.

And may we all rise as the resurrected, the awakened, the fearless lovers of the One who first loved us.

this is my story. this is my song
Praising my Savior all the day long.

You are
cordially invited
to take your seat
at the table

Come to the Table

To all the beautiful women who have forgotten the sacred art of coming to the table—to share our lives, our laughter, our wounds, our wisdom—there's a special seat waiting just for **you**.

And for every relationship that's been forged in love, struggle, and truth, there's space too.

There's something holy about a community of like-hearted women who are brave enough to share their dreams, their hopes, their failures, and their victories.

The collective beauty that gathers around that table is **sacred**—and when we come together in authenticity, it's **transformative**.

Each chair at this table has been placed with intention by the Maker of Life Himself. And there is always a seat re-served for **Him**. He is our center. Our common ground. Our dream-giver. Our constant. The thread woven through each of our individual expressions. The Giver of Life.

Sometimes I see myself following others through this breathtaking terrain—through a wooden canopy that opens into a clearing where a long, simple, beautiful table waits. I watch as I take my seat while others are still gathering.

There is no fear here, no anxiety—just peace. Anticipation. Wholeness.

ife is like food—meant to be **shared**. When we open our hearts, when we're no longer afraid of being seen, we offer the real bread and wine of our lives. Just as **He** once did, so should we.

This is communion. The sacred act of sharing stories, laughter, tears, and dreams. The sacred exchange of the bread and blood of our journeys.

As I sit there, I remember those who've gone before—those who are no longer here, yet remain so very present. They've crossed just beyond the veil, but they still gather with us. They still speak. Still walk beside us. Still partake in all that we've lived and loved.

If I look closely, I can almost see them.
The ones who spoke life into our hearts.
The ones who helped shape who we are.
They are still with us—here, at the table.

o come.
Come to the table with me.
Let's remember. Let's feast. Let's dream again.
Let's make room for one another—and for Him.

Birth Story
Natural & Spiritual Inheritance

My birth story is one for the books.

My mother's journey through childbirth was marked by both suffering and strength. Her first child—a baby boy—was born in the country, where hospitals were scarce and the only person available to assist was the town veterinarian. It's a heartbreaking story. The baby was breech, and the vet, doing what he could, pulled him out feet first. He lived only a day and a half. The loss pierced their hearts.

Then came my sister, Deanna—ten years older than me. Her birth was uneventful, a brief moment of light. But after that, a long shadow fell. Over the next nine years, my mother suffered seven miscarriages. Seven children whose names were never spoken, yet who surely sing in the halls of heaven. And then—me.

My parents, desperate and full of faith, attended one of Oral Roberts' healing crusades. They were prayed over, and a prophetic word came forth—a child was coming. They believed it would be a boy. Back then, boys were expected to carry the mantle. But God had something different in mind.

During the early months of my mother's pregnancy, the old pattern began to repeat—complications, fear, the slow weight of dread. But the church intercessors rose up, determined to see this one through.

A woman named Ruth Jones in particular—a fierce, faithful intercessor—became a spiritual midwife. She prayed day and night, stood beside my mother through it all. Ruth became a spiritual mother to me long before I was born.

I truly believe prayer shaped me before breath ever entered my lungs. I was carried on intercession, cradled in the womb by faith. My spiritual DNA is steeped in that kind of devotion. I was bathed in prayer—surrounded by the rhythm of heaven, the whisper of women who refused to let go.

When I arrived, it wasn't the boy they expected. There was some surprise in the room. If I had been a boy, my name was to be Oral—after Oral Roberts. But instead, my mother named me Bonita, after the movie star Bonita Granville, and gave me a feminized version of Oral—Oralaine.
So, I came into this world carrying the names of a film star and a healing evangelist: Bonita Oralaine Kitchen, born on July 17, 1953.

But the story doesn't end there. When I was four, my mother conceived again. This time, everything seemed to go well. She carried the baby to term. But just two days before the due date, the heartbeat was gone. My sister was stillborn. I remember seeing her—a beautiful baby girl with a head full of black hair. That loss devastated my mother. Some griefs leave a mark that never quite fades.

Years later, in prayer, I caught a glimpse of her in heaven – surrounded by all her children, laughing, whole, full of peace. That picture stays with me. It brings comfort.

You see, I was one of the ones who made it. And some-times I wonder: Was the inheritance meant for all of us? Did it fall on me and Deanna to carry what was planted in our family line—the promises, the prophetic words, the destiny etched into our scrolls? Life hasn't been easy. But I've come through with strength forged in the fire and a heart marked by grace.

The legacy Heaven wrote for me is still unfolding. I am more aware than ever that my birth was not an accident. Heaven rejoiced when I arrived. It didn't turn out like I imagined—but the journey has been full of love, mystery, and the deep knowing of the One who loved me first.

It's good to remember where we come from. Our roots tell us more than we realize. And mine? They are anchored in loss, love, and the relentless prayers of women who refused to let go of promise.

holding to the promise
journey into love

strength forged in fire
heart marked by grace

Woven by Design

Before I formed you in the womb I knew you,
and before you were born I set you apart...
– Jeremiah 1:5

Some connections are ancient.
Older than our memories, deeper than our logic.
They were written in the heart of God
before time began.
Every reunion, every divine encounter,
is a thread pulled through eternity—
a whisper of heaven meeting earth again.

We do not walk by chance.
We walk by design.

The Airlines
&
The God Who Knows

The song played in my head as my life took a turn I never expected.

It all started with Debbie. My friend. She had just started working for American West Airlines and wanted me to interview. I said no—I didn't want anything to do with a 24/7 job. But Debbie was relentless.

"Just apply," she said. "Let's travel the world"

The idea of seeing the world was tempting, but that schedule? No thanks.

Still, she wore me down. Finally, just to get her off my back, I said yes—fully expecting *not* to be hired.

I showed up for the interview. There were about forty other applicants, many with degrees or airline school credentials. When it was my turn to introduce myself, I thought, *What do I have to lose?* There's no way I'm getting this job.

But then something unexpected happened—**they called my name for a second interview.**

Favor.

Then a third.

When God opens a door, no man can shut it.

The third interview included a hearing test, eye exam, a lifting requirement… and the dreaded typing test. This wasn't a computer-based test—it was an *actual typewriter* test. They sat me next to a woman who typed 70 words a minute. Her fingers were flying, the bell dinging with every new line. I couldn't concentrate. My fingers froze.

I failed. By two words.

I needed 26 words per minute and typed 24.

The instructor looked at me and said, "What happened?"

"She was typing so fast next to me!" I told her. "I couldn't think!"

She looked at me and said, "Come back during my lunch break. I'll test you alone."

Who does that?

Only God can orchestrate something so small and so specific. Sure enough, I came back, passed the test, and was hired.

What I didn't know then was how much of a lifeline this job would be for me and my family. It gave us access when my husband worked out of town. It allowed me to go on mission trips around the world. It even helped me visit my kids when we were living in different places.

od knew what I needed before I did. The job was a *gift*. But one day, He asked me to give it up.

That was a hard one.

Airline jobs don't pay much, but the benefits are amazing. I had planned to stay until I could retire with lifetime perks. But in **September 2000**, the Lord spoke clearly:

"This will be your last year with the airline."

I was devastated. "Lord, how could You ask me to give this up? I've worked so hard!"

But eventually, after much fussing at Him, I surrendered.

Time passed, and I honestly forgot what He had said. Then September came around again. I was in Romania on a mission trip with a team… and **9/11 happened.**

All travel stopped. Fear spread. But honestly, we were safer in Romania than in the U.S.

While there, the Lord reminded me of His word:

"Do you remember what I told you?"

"Yes," I answered, heart sinking.

"This is the time."

I thought my missionary days were over. I grieved. I was sad.

But when I got home, something incredible happened.

The airline offered an **early retirement program**—the exact thing I would have needed to walk away without losing my benefits. The industry had been hit hard and needed to downsize. I asked the Lord, "Is this it?" He said, "Yes."

And just like that—the very thing I thought I'd lose, He *gave back* to me. I got to retire a year after He first spoke it, three years earlier than planned, and **I kept all my benefits.**

I repented for my ugly attitude.

But He understood.

He had a plan.

He was teaching me to **TRUST.**

And trust I did.

What a *big* God we serve.

A God who sees what we don't.

A God who asks us to surrender—and then meets us with something better.

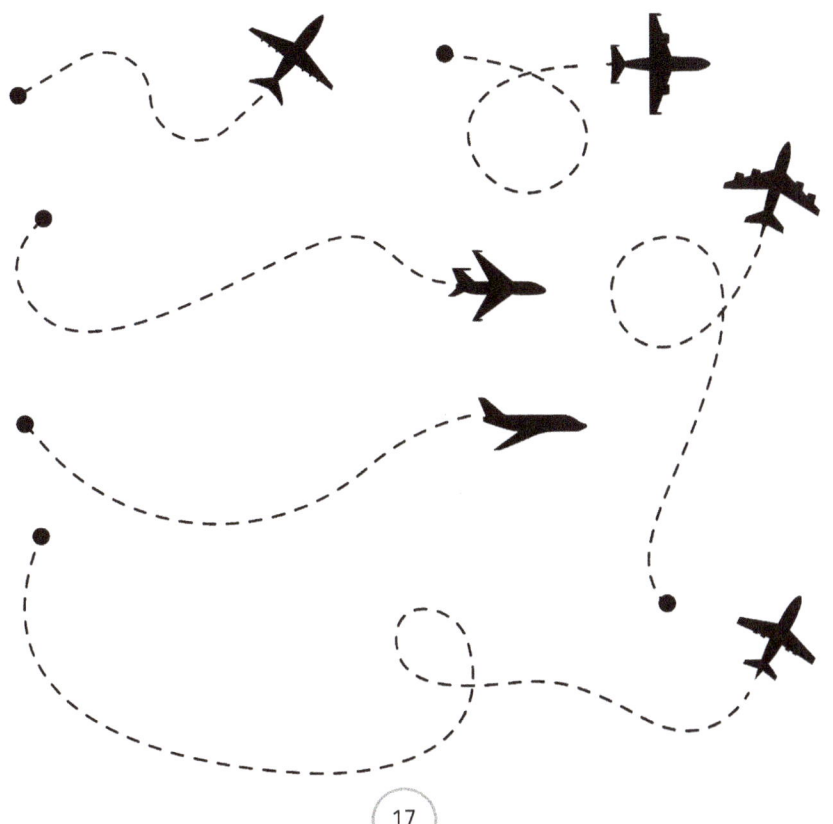

The Sound of Paper

The journey didn't start with a book.

It started with a whisper. A tug. Something I couldn't ignore.

I knew there were books inside me—stories, encounters, sacred moments—but fear had a grip on me. I had heard prophetic words spoken over my life, calling me a writer, a voice, but I didn't really *believe* them. Not yet.

You see, there was a time when even speaking in front of others was terrifying. Singing? Impossible. I was locked in a silence I had agreed with—built on the belief that I wasn't good enough. That my voice didn't matter. That I had nothing worth saying. Agreement is a powerful tool.

That silence became my prison. A false shelter built on fear and unworthiness.

But healing and love doesn't leave us alone.

Years passed. Inner work is being done. Lies were ex-
posed. And something sacred started to stir. I took a risk.
I said yes to a tiny spark of courage and formed a small
group—a circle of unwritten, unpublished writers. We came
together not to impress, but to be honest. To show up.
To speak. To write.

I named it The Sound of Paper.

Because I believed—even in my trembling—that paper could
carry sound. That our words could come alive, the living
word to speak truth, create beauty, and carry healing. That
the act of writing could unlock what fear had tried to silence.

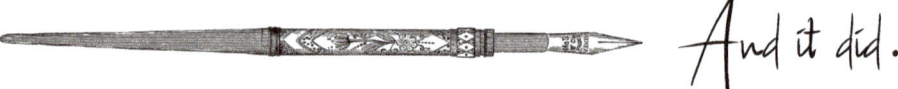 And it did.

What began as a support group became an ignition point.
A fire was kindled. Stories started to rise. Not perfect. Not
polished. But *alive*. Our pens moved, and each time we
met our voices grew stronger.

This book is born from that leap.

I write now because I realized my stories, my encounters,
my sacred wrestling with God—they have a voice. A voice
that changed my life. And maybe, just maybe, these words
will change someone else's, too.

Because our lives are not random. They're sacred journeys.

His stories written in us.

We are meant to share them. Taste them. Witness them.

Living epistles written in our hearts,

known and read by all men,

Not written on tablets of stone,

but in fleshly tablets

of the heart.

2 CORINTHIANS. 3:2-3

So come.

Taste and see. Let His goodness awaken in your life. Let it take shape—in poetry, in story, in silence, in song. Let your life speak. Let the sound of paper be heard again.

Because He is good.

And so are you.

AcTivAtIoN

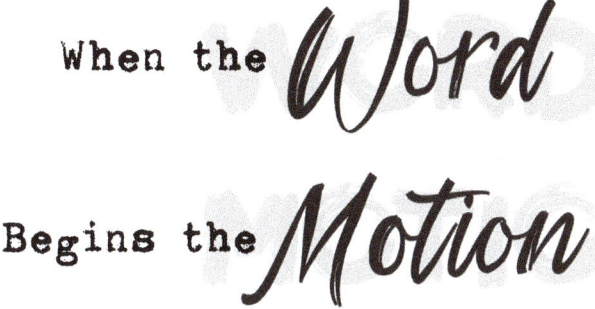

When the *Word*

Begins the *Motion*

It's the act of starting something. Making it work. Setting it into motion.

A word is released—and suddenly, things shift. Wheels begin to turn. The engine of destiny revs to life, and without realizing it, we are launched.

And most of the time, we don't even see it in the moment. It's only in hindsight that we realize: *That was it. That was the word. That was the beginning.*

For me, it started at the Deep Dive, early in the year. When Darla gave me my Hebraic birth portion and spoke it over me, I heard it loud and clear: *words, words, words*—they were the essence of my scroll. And something inside me said, yes. I'd known it all along. That moment didn't just affirm what I carried—it *activated* it.

That word unlocked the courage to begin. To write. To risk. To put pen to page and dare to believe that what's inside of me is holy, worth expressing, and waiting to be harvested.

Now, here I am – midway through the journey – and I'm seeing it clearly: **WORDS CREATE WORLDS.**

By faith we understand that the universe was formed at God's command, so that what is seen was not made out of what was visible. Hebrews 11:3

Creation itself was activated by a voice. And so are we.

We carry that same power. The words we speak don't just describe our reality—they shape it. They charge the air with purpose, call things into being, and open scrolls that were sealed.

That's why this book matters. Not because it's perfect or polished—but because it is spoken. It's a response. An act of faith. A manifestation of the frequency that was planted in me from the beginning.

And I believe it's just the beginning.

So here's the question:

WHAT WORD HAS BEEN SPOKEN OVER YOU?

What phrase, what truth, what divine echo stirred something so deep you couldn't un-hear it?

Because that might just be your activation. And once it begins, there's no going back!

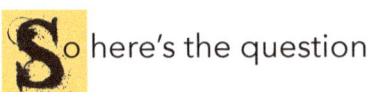

```
Your word have I hidden in my heart...
```

INFINITELY

INFINITE

INFINITY

The big, black Cadillac

Have you ever been lost—not just geographically, but so lost you didn't even recognize yourself? I have.

There was a time when I stood at a real crossroads in life. Who I was, where I'd been, where I was going—none of it made sense anymore. And to say I was "lost" doesn't even begin to describe it. I was lost *inside* myself. My identity? Gone. My tribe? Gone. My marriage? Gone. I was completely and utterly lost…

Until one day, a **big black Cadillac** arrived.

*I*n my encounter, I was standing on a street corner, frantically searching for my phone so I could call someone—anyone. I just needed someone to know where I was. But the phone was nowhere to be found. I remember running from a tall three-story building, desperate to find what I had been made for. For two years, I'd been haunted by one question—*"Are you going to follow Me, or them?"*

That day, the question became a command:

"Make a decision—Me or them."

I knew in that moment I had to choose *Him*. Deep down, I knew it was going to be a rough road. The "them" had stood by me through some of the hardest times of my life, and I was grateful. But in that place, I had lost the essence of *me*. I was trying to be someone I wasn't.

So, I chose Him. And everything changed.

It's funny where life takes us—so many paths, so many turns. But all roads lead back to Him. The search for purpose never ends, I'm convinced of that. But we have this promise: **He works all things together for our good.**

As I stood there—stranded and alone—wondering if anyone knew where I was, out of nowhere, this **big black Cadillac** pulled up. A man stepped out of the driver's seat and said, **"We're here to pick you up."**

The Cadillac had big fins on the back—classic and commanding. As I walked toward the car, I noticed others inside. I slid in on the driver's side into the long, old-fashioned bench seat and sat next to *JoAnn*. In the back seat were Christine, Susi and Don. Once I was settled, Susi reached up behind me and handed me what I thought was my missing phone.

I said, "Oh! There's my phone." She replied, "No. This is a *receiver.* It belongs to you."

Then the woman next to me handed me two CDs. One was wrapped in lace—feminine and intimate. The other was artsy and bold. She looked at me and said,

"These belong to you."

What struck me was that I knew of these people in real life—but had never met them personally. Yet here they were, in the car, handing me things that felt deeply significant.

And then, the man who'd stepped out to get me sat down next to me. He smiled, put the pedal to the metal, and off we went. That man was the Lord Himself. He knew exactly where I was—and who to bring with Him.

You see, earlier in my life, I had been asked by that same voice, **"What do you want?"**

I always answered, "I want my family to know You." But that day, He asked again, *"No—what do **you** want?"*

I didn't know how to answer. I kept turning the question back to Him, "What do you want?" But again, He pushed: "What do you want?"

Finally, in frustration, I said, **"Fine! I want to know the anointing Christine carries in intercession. And I want to know worship like Don carries!"**

And then I heard it—clear as day: **"DONE."**

It shocked me. It was as if He'd just been waiting for me to acknowledge the cry of my own heart. To own it. And once I did, it was *finished*—already done. And now, in that car with me? Christine and Don. I hadn't met them at the time of that prayer. But there they were.

The woman sitting beside me—the one who handed me the CDs—is someone I've long admired. A pioneer in the Kingdom. Fearless. Prophetic. A true songbird whose calling has literally changed history. Our story continues in another chapter, but her presence in that moment was profound. I honor and love her deeply.

Every person in that car had played a part in the story God was unfolding for me. And the Lord was showing me— **this is your future.** This is what happens when you choose Me. Your **yes** opens My heart.

He'll do that for all of us—when we give Him our yes.

Oh, I have many more stories about the beautiful and unexpected paths He's led me down… but the Big Black Cadillac? That one I'll never forget.

If we let Him drive—if we let Him take us where only He knows we need to go—He will open worlds and realms we could never imagine.

"Eye has not seen, ear has not heard, nor has it entered into the heart of man what God has prepared for those who love Him."

So come on.

Let's go take a ride in His Big Black Cadillac.

Apparently…He really likes that car.

Fragrance
of
Remembrance

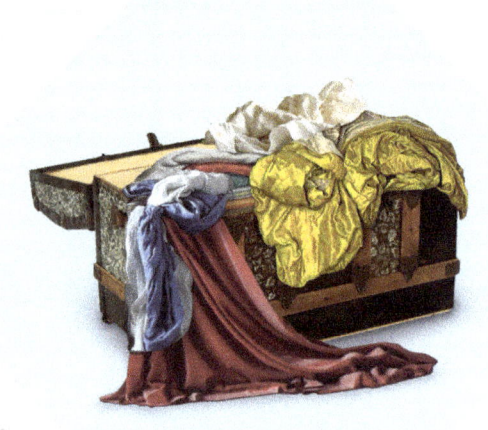

As I opened the chest, I could feel my heart pounding—uncertain, afraid, not knowing what might be inside.

Fabric began to billow out, swirling and alive with movement. It moved and as though it had a purpose of its own.

Why fabric? I thought. I came seeking answers… my hopes, my dreams… but all I see is fabric?

In the background, I could hear His voice. Faint, but insistent. Echoing from somewhere beyond the veil of time and memory.

"You may have forgotten, but I have not."

Over and over again, the words came. A whisper…

"You may have forgotten… but I have not."

I knelt there, with my gaze upon the fabric, by the chest, with the voice still softly speaking. And suddenly, I remembered how I got here.

A few weeks earlier, He had asked me to come, as I stood in the hallway, I saw Him standing in a room—dusty, empty, echoing with silence—beside the old hope chest. I had known instantly what this place was. Not just a physical room, but something deeper.

It was a room I had abandoned.

A place I had locked away, hidden behind a door I'd slammed shut long ago. A room in my heart that I had once lived in—and fled.

t felt as real as the walls of my home, but I knew it lived inside me.

Dust covered everything. Light streamed in through the windows in light beams, soft but unwavering. A few pieces of furniture remained, cast-offs from another life. There was even a toppled chair, lying on its side as if someone had left in a rush…

The realization hit me. This was the room of my divorce.

All the pain. The disillusionment. The promises that were broken and dreams undone. It was too much to carry, too much to face. So, I did what I had to do.

I left. I closed the door. I shut it down.

But He hadn't.

He remembered.

And now, so did I.

I remember standing in the hallway, watching myself open the hope chest.

When He first appeared to me—standing in that room, beside the chest—I couldn't bring myself to go to Him. He called to me again and again, gently urging me forward… but I was afraid. Afraid of what I might find. After that first encounter, my heart sank… I repented for my fear, and then the peace of God swept over my soul.

And now, days later, here I am again—taken someplace outside of time—watching myself open it.

*W*hat caught me off guard were the fabrics. So many fabrics.

Why fabrics? I asked.

He smiled, with a quiet knowing.

"This is the fabric of your life," He said. **"Colorful, beautiful—not only to the eye, but to the touch."**

He was showing me, me.

Each piece was alive. Vibrant. Sacred. A living record of who I was. I felt the truth of this deep down. I was amazed. These fabrics spoke to my DNA—the very Ruach breath of creation in which I was made.

I reached out and gathered them in my arms. I pressed them to my face and began to breathe them in. And as I did, the fragrance of remembrance filled me.

The more I breathed, the more I remembered Him.

His essence. His presence. It was intoxicating.

Something deeper began to happen.. The more I remembered Him, I began to remember me. *The more I breathed Him in, the more I was remembering me* - not only back to *Him*, but also back to myself.

And then I knew: we had never truly been apart. We had always been one.

I had always been in Him.

Since the very beginning.

*I*t reminded me of Job, when God said, *"Where were you when I laid the foundations of the earth? When I hung the moon and the stars?"*

And the truth struck me with clarity—I had been there.

I was a witness.

I had simply forgotten.

Like Job, I had forgotten who I was… and where I had come from. How can I forget something like that? Life's journey can cloud the very essence I was made for.

But now I remembered: I was there, before time. Before this earth. Before this body—this earth suit—I was spirit.

I had always been spirit.

And I was returning to the truth of who I had always been.

It was a strange resolve. Within the fragrance of remembrance it seemed to erase all my fears and confusion about my divorce…

Even though I didn't fully understand why my marriage ended, I knew He knew—and that in time, He would reveal it to me.

I had been the one to say, *"I'll never get a divorce. It goes against everything I believe in."* There had been years of prayers sown, faith beyond measure, promises made by so many about the beauty that would come. My life had hung on that promise—on the belief that love, faith, and perseverance would see us through. But in the end, the weight of irreconcilable differences had claimed its victory.

We had grown so far apart, even though we still loved each other. There had been a time when I thought recovery was possible, when hope flickered—until this.

His words, *"You may have forgotten, but I have not,"* carried a weight that I hadn't expected. It hit me hard because I had pushed aside every hope I ever had of a beautiful marriage. I had abandoned the belief that restoration was even possible. But He hadn't forgotten. Not the prayers. Not the faith. Not the promises I had made, or the beauty we once shared.

Even though the ending didn't make sense—*even though it hurt beyond words*—in that moment, it was enough to know that *He knew*… and hadn't forgotten.

It's funny how that happens. Just the acknowledgment that He knew—that He remembered—was enough to begin a quiet reconciliation in my heart.

His fragrance was so powerful, it brought the healing remembrance I so desperately needed.

In the act of remembering, I didn't just recall the Father God of the universe. Wrapped up inside of Him, I also remembered *me*—who I was, and where it all began. That moment revealed the framework of not only myself, but the very foundation of the world.

I don't know why He came to me like this, but the way He revealed Himself spoke to the deepest part of my heart. He had known me then, and He knows me now.

We were one, and we still are. Nothing—*nothing*—can separate us from the love of God.

It became clear to me that He is here with me, moment by moment, minute by minute, hour by hour, and day by day. His love overshadows any hardship I will ever walk through. Just knowing He's here, that He knows, and that He's on the job—maybe that's what spoke to me most of all.

He's got this.

He's got me. He's got my circumstances. He's got my life. Whatever comes next—it's all His.

He's never forsaken me. He's never left.

I may have forgotten… but He has not.

And the fragrance He brings will not only cause us to remember who we are, but also *remember Him.*

Sometimes, it's good to just sit.

Sit with whatever is going on in our lives.
No fixing, no striving—just be aware.
Feel, if we can.

For so long, we've been taught to dismiss pain,
to figure it out, to fret, to fight—even to warfare
our way out of what's hard.

But what if...
What if we just be still and know?

What if we simply allow God to reveal what He
wants to reveal—in His time?

If He holds our days, our times, our moments...
then nothing surprises Him.
Nothing.

He's not in the heavens wringing His hands in worry.
He's not pacing the throne room.
He's got this.

Literally —
        He's got the whole world in His hands.

And that is where we enter His rest:
Not by understanding, but by knowing
—deep in our bones—that He's in control.

He truly has the whole world in His hands.

Peace

"I leave the gift of peace with you — my peace.
Not the kind of fragile peace given by the world,
but my perfect peace. Don't yield to fear or be
troubled in your hearts — instead, be courageous!

John 14:27

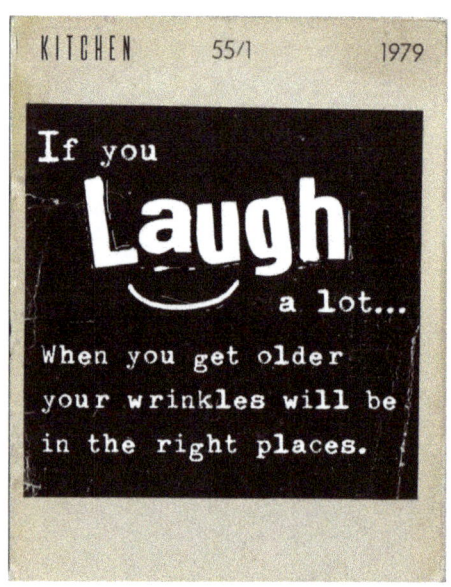

*A HAPPY HEART is good medicine
and a joyful mind causes healing,
but a broken spirit dries up the bones. — Proverbs 17:22*

THE HEALING SOUND
OF LAUGHTER

I love to laugh. Really laugh. The kind that bubbles up unexpectedly, the kind that hijacks your breath and waters your eyes and at times makes you run to the bathroom! I have this friend—my best laughing buddy—and when we're together, the joy flows freely. It's like our eyes catch the same odd or hilarious thing at the exact same moment. We don't need words. One glance, and we're both doubled over in contagious, uncontrollable laughter.

Our families and friends know this about us. They just smile, shake their heads, and say, *"There they go again."* And somehow, that makes it even funnier.

But our laughter isn't rooted in sarcasm or at anyone's expense—it's joy in its purest form. Unfiltered. Unifying. Healing. A reminder that God created joy, and He delights when we step into it.

One day, I heard the Lord laugh. It was deep, like a big belly laugh, rich and full, echoing through the atmosphere with divine authority. I was lying in my room, feeling uneasy after sensing something dark nearby, when suddenly–His laughter broke through. It wasn't just comforting–it was *warfare*. That laugh sent demonic forces scattering. They couldn't stand the sound of it. It carried weight, frequency, and power. In that moment, I realized: even God's joy is a weapon. His presence, His peace, His laughter – they carry undeniable dominion.

The beginning, the end, and all the in-betweens. He's not disturbed by the chaos we see; He already has the outcome in mind.

So now, when I laugh with my friend, I see it differently. It's not just a moment of humor. It's a gift. A glimpse into heaven's lightness. A reminder that joy isn't weak– it's *holy*. It's part of the Kingdom. It pushes back darkness. It renews our minds. It heals our bones.

Ronda, may we never ever stop laughing!

A glance. a nod. no words required.

In silent talks. we're both inspired.

Ronda knows. without a cue.

exactly what I'm going through.

The Place Beautiful

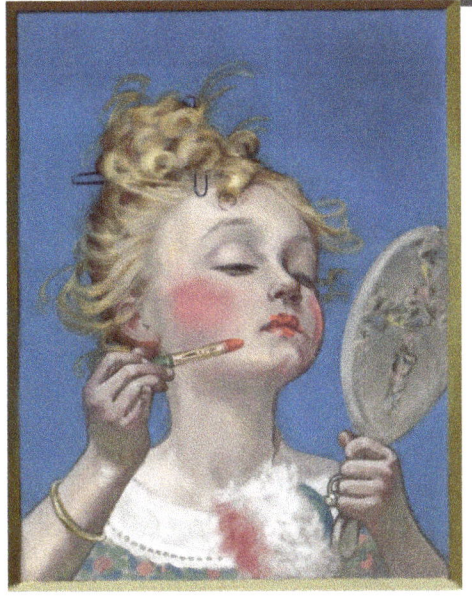

Being seen for who we truly are—that's where freedom begins.

Sometimes I hear someone speak and their words hit with the weight of truth—they pack a punch because they're *real*. Other times, I hear words that land flat, hollow, lifeless. I wonder… do they even believe what they're saying?

What would happen if we all spoke from the place of *truth*? If we dared to speak authentically—with masks off and hearts open?

I wonder how much healing would begin to unravel in our hearts, minds, and souls if we simply had the courage to be real—with ourselves, and with each other.

Because at the heart of the matter—that's what really counts.

Maybe our healing would accelerate. Maybe we'd stop hiding behind polished created personas. I'm not talking about being brash or cruel in the name of "just telling it like it is." No—real truth doesn't destroy. Real truth carries the quiet power of brokenness laid bare… unashamed, unhidden.

Not to shame, but to set others free.

When we're honest with ourselves, we open a door—one others can walk through too. Our healing becomes a *pathway*, a living invitation. As we walk in truth, fear loses its grip. Courage rises. Wholeness follows.

This is the place where God meets us—the sacred ground of authenticity. Where we dare to stand before Him, eye to eye, and begin to see what He sees in us.

The Place Beautiful.

He calls us lovely. He calls us beautiful. He only sees Himself in us.

The Song of Songs comes to mind. He doesn't criticize or count our past—He gazes with love and says:
s*"How beautiful you are, my darling… your eyes are like doves."* Eyes of gentleness. Purity. Innocence. Love.

That's what He sees.

No matter where we come from, no matter what we've walked through—He sees us through eyes of perfect love.

And that changes *everything*.

Perfect

The Land, the Treasure & the Harvester

I was reminded of a dream I had years ago.

I stood before a parcel of land, golden and ripe with wheat. The field was mine—and was full of life. Surrounding it was untouched earth. But this portion—this field—had been planted, nurtured, and now stood ready for harvest.

At the front of the field stood a large angelic figure. He wore overalls, his presence earthy yet radiant, heaven and humanity woven together. His hair shimmered like living light, golden and in motion. There was joy on his face—a smile that strangely reminded me of Jiminy Cricket. A moral compass. A guide. A friend. The conscience of a boy who longed to be real.

Wow, that'll preach!

This angel was the harvester. Strong. Sure. And smiling wide—because the field was ready.

As I recall this dream, I realize: this is not just a dream of harvest, but of **ownership**. The land had been entrusted to me. The wheat had grown under my care, even if unconsciously. And yet,

beyond that golden field, there was more land—
still mine—but unplanted. Untouched. Waiting.

We each have a field on this earth. A place of divine
appointment. A territory meant to bear fruit. But do
we know what lies buried within it?

> *The kingdom of heaven is like a very precious*
> *treasure hidden in a field. Which a man found*
> *and hid again; then in his joy he goes and sells*
> *all he has and buys that field (securing the*
> *treasure for himself).* – Matthew 13:44

The kingdom is hidden in the land. The treasure
requires risk, sacrifice, a full YES. That man gave up
everything to possess the field—not just the treasure.
Because the treasure and the field cannot be separated.

> *There is treasure inside us—placed in earthen*
> *vessels so that the surpassing glory would be*
> *of God and not of us* – 2 Corinthians 4:7

The wheat in the dream speaks of bread—living bread.
The fragrance of fresh-baked bread, Yeshua Himself.
Something the world cannot resist. Something nourish-
ing, that sustains us and is eternal.

This book—this act of writing—is part of that harvest.
It is me saying yes. Me risking it all to bring forth what
He planted.

To reap what I didn't even fully realize was growing.

And there is still land yet to be planted. Still promises unfolding. Still secrets to discover.

So here is the sacred question:

Are you willing to sell all and buy the field of your heart?

Because it is *there* that the kingdom lies buried.

We are stepping into days of discovery—days when divine grace pulls back the veil. We're being invited to uncover who we are, what we love, and why we were made. There is a call rising: **Go buy the field.** All of it. Plant. Wait. Harvest.

There is a treasure within.

And heaven is smiling, waiting with overalls and radiant hair, because the harvest is coming.

Sacred
Connections

There's a knowing that lives deep in the spirit. It by-passes the mind, the logic, the calendar—and when it stirs, you feel it like a whisper inside your bones. That's how I've begun to recognize the ones God has placed in my path. Not as strangers, not as random acquaintances, but as **divine appointments**—threads in the tapestry He's been weaving all along.

These are not chance meetings. They are sacred collisions.

Sometimes I meet someone, and it feels like they've been with me all along. I can't explain it in natural terms. There's a stirring, a flicker, something in me that lights up—like a match being struck in a dark room. I may not understand what they carry for me, or what I carry for them, but my spirit knows: this one is part of the journey.

It's a dance of sorts—a **spirit dance**. Not choreo-graphed by human design, but orchestrated by heaven. And for far too long, I'd stand on the edges of that dance, afraid to step in. Shyness. Insecurity. The voice in my head whispering, *Why would they want to know you?* So I'd stay back, hesitate, miss moments. But I'm learning now that when the Spirit draws, it's not just for me—it's for what's meant to come alive between us.

There's purpose in these connections. Sometimes, we see it right away. Other times, it unfolds slowly—decades later, even. I once knew a woman at a church I used to attend. We were never close, not really. Just polite. But deep inside, I saw her as a friend, someone I knew. It didn't make sense at the time, but the feeling never left me. Then twenty years passed.

One day, out of nowhere, we crossed paths again—and the knowing returned. Strong. Clear. Unshakable. What I had sensed back then came into bloom. She became the friend I always saw her to be. Time had only matured the connection. It wasn't delayed; it was destined—just not for then. It was for the *now*.

That's the mystery I'm seeing more and more—**God's orchestration** of people, places, and timing. Some connections are for a season. Others are covenant. And sometimes, He withholds a relationship to protect what we're not ready to steward. But when it's time, He brings us back to each other like threads finally pulling tight.

I believe if we could trace the map of our lives with spiritual eyes, we'd see the hidden stitching—the divine design. The people who enter, exit, return, or remain—they are part of His weaving. Part of the glory. We are not meant to walk alone. And in the Kingdom, relationship is never just about comfort—it's about **calling**.

So now, when that feeling rises in me—the deep draw, the quiet recognition—I lean in.

I ask God,

What are You doing — here?

What do You want to grow between us?

I don't want to miss a single thread He's trying to sew.

Because what once felt random, I now know to be sacred.

Sacred

To everything. turn. turn. turn
There is a season. turn. turn. turn
And a time to every purpose under heaven
A time to be born. a time to die
A time to plant. a time to reap
A time to kill. a time to heal
A time to laugh. a time to weep

A TIME TO TURN

"To everything there is a season, and a time to every purpose under heaven." – Ecclesiastes 3:1

The words of Scripture, echoed in this timeless song, remind us that life is not random—it is patterned with holy timing. There are seasons to build and seasons to break down. Times of mourning and times of dancing. Moments to hold close and moments to let go.

If we're not careful, we rush through it all—resisting the breaking-down seasons, clinging too tightly in the letting-go ones, and missing the quiet beauty hidden in each appointed time.

But if we stop, if we turn, we begin to see it:
God's fingerprints in our waiting.
His mercy in our undoing.
His promise in every new beginning.

Even if you feel like you've missed your moment, even if you're in a hard place right now, hear this:

It's not too late.

The One who holds every season is also holding you.

Scroll, Walker

Little did I know when that Cadillac rolled up what heaven had just sent into my life.

Remember that prayer I prayed—the one where the Lord said **"Done"**? Well, let me tell you—He knows *exactly* who to send. My desire had matched His, and He just needed my agreement.

I met Christine during a worship school in Redding, California. While there, I had several vivid dreams. I didn't know what they meant, but Christine did. That's how she was—tuned in, sharp, discerning. She told me the dreams were significant for the school. I didn't have a clue what I was carrying, but she saw it. Isn't that just like God? We just walk into things—"Cadillacing" along—and He starts revealing His strategies.

Christine and Don were *legends* in the worship movement. Don's worship through MorningStar changed the atmosphere of the entire church age, and Christine—right behind him—engaged in heaven with prophetic movement and fierce intercession. That era was drenched in presence… Heaven literally invaded earth through sound, motion, and prayer. They weren't just ministers—they were scroll-walkers. That school *wrecked* me—in the best way possible. It was warfare. It was healing. It was legacy.

That prayer I had prayed?
This was the answer.

e aligned me with kingdom purpose in ways I could never have orchestrated on my own. Even though I didn't understand it all, I walked it out anyway.

After class one day, Christine asked if I wanted to join them for dinner. I said yes, of course! But it wasn't until dessert came that I knew they were my tribe. Something about sharing one dessert plate—that table of communion—sealed it for me. It felt like family.

At the end of that school, Christine said, *"Let's stay in touch."* I was elated. I later invited them to Arizona for a worship conference, and they said yes—**when the time was right**. That's the Potters—never rushing anything. They taught me the discipline of *waiting on God*. Timing is everything in the kingdom.

Eventually, they came. And when they stayed at my house, Christine looked around and asked, *"Do you live like this?"* I had made everything spotless, like a model home— trying to impress. But I knew what she meant. She was asking, *Where's the real you?*
I laughed and said, *"Not all the time!"*
She let out a big sigh of relief.
I had passed the test.
Christine was always searching for *authenticity*.

Every morning, we'd sit on my couch, and she would begin to teach me. She became my rabbi, schooling me in the kingdom. She dismantled religious boxes and opened prison doors I didn't even know I was locked inside of. This was not long after my divorce—I was raw, tender, and stepping into a new season. And God sent me the best.

on and Christine carried the Father's and Mother's hearts of the kingdom. They nurtured me. Poured into me. And one day, after that conference, they invited me to come live with them. I was shocked—and deeply honored. *"It's a new day,"* Christine said.

A new season was beginning.

Markers. Markers. And more markers.
He establishes what He has in store.

My time with the Potters changed my life. Some of the most exhilarating and painful moments happened in that season. They helped me walk out of fear. I remember one intercession where I had completely lost my voice. Christine began to scream while I sobbed uncontrollably. I couldn't release—but she released for me. That's who she was—a priest, a midwife, a covering. She went deep, always Spirit-led, always tuned in to heaven.

They introduced me to Bob Jones—another marker.
One day at his house, as we were leaving, we stood in the driveway and were surrounded by the strongest scent of roses. Bob pointed at me and said:

"That's you. That's you. You'll be the fragrance of life to some—and the fragrance of death to others."

He was quoting 2 Corinthians 2:16:

To the one, we are the aroma of death leading to death, and to the other, the aroma of life leading to life. And who is sufficient for these things?

The rose has been a recurring theme in my life ever since. And the Potters knew how to draw that fragrance out of me.

I was like their spiritual daughter during that time—nurtured, cared for, championed. And Don—what a father. Every time I picked them up at the airport, he'd ask, *"Are you okay?"*

Every time, I'd cry. And he'd hug me and breathe life back into me. A true seer. A father. A chief musician of his time.

There are so many more stories—too many to name here. But I think you get the drift. They were family. They were my **divine alignment**.

And you see—it all began with my **yes**.

I'll preach this to my dying day:
All God needs is our yes.
Our agreement.
Our full surrender.

When we give Him that—He does the rest.
He brings the impossible.
He sends the extravagant gifts.
He gives us the keys of the kingdom.

And oh—how we need them.

The Tunnel

Have you ever found yourself in a situation where you had no idea what was about to happen?

I have.

It was one of the first times I'd been invited to travel with Don and Christine to a conference. The speaker was a man named Paul Cox—someone unlike anyone I had ever encountered. I didn't know what to expect. He wasn't flashy or loud, but he carried something. You could feel it.

One by one, he met with us individually. When it was my turn, I sat down across from him, still green, still unsure of myself. He looked at me and said, plainly, "I see depression."

What?

My thoughts were, You just met me. And that's the first thing out of your mouth?

I was stunned—but I couldn't deny it. Not really. I had buried so much—grief, fear, pain, fatigue. I had learned to put on a brave face, but inside, I was worn thin.

 Then he prayed.

And as he prayed, something happened. I was no longer in that room.

I was being propelled through a long hallway–like a tunnel–and people stood on either side of it, lining the path. They were cheering. Speaking with weight and authority: "We've been waiting for this." Over and over again: "We've been waiting for this."

It was like my spirit was being launched forward, pushed into something ancient and destined.

I didn't tell anyone what happened. I was too afraid. What if I got it wrong? What if I was just making it up? In those days, I second-guessed everything. My voice was still shaking its way out of the silence it had lived under for too long.

But I never forgot that tunnel.

Never forgot those voices cheering me on.

Never forgot the sense that it wasn't just about me–that I was somehow saying yes for the ones who had gone before, and for the ones still to come.

Here's why I'm telling you this: because fear has a way of locking us down. Shame will silence you. But God–He walks us out of those strongholds, one step at a time. He opens doors we thought were sealed shut. And sometimes, He uses unlikely people to hold the keys.

My journey hasn't been neat or predictable. It's been extreme at times—messy, raw, wild. But I'm still walking it out. I'm learning. I'm healing.

Even writing this book is a victory. A long, hard-won yes.

Because putting my life on paper—the unfiltered, unvarnished story—is part of my healing. It's my offering. My drink poured out for those who thirst. The Book of Bonita—flawed, holy, unfinished.

There's power in our testimonies. That's why I write.

Isaiah 58:12 has become my cornerstone:

"And your people will rebuild the ancient ruins;
You will raise up and restore the age-old foundations;
You will be called Repairer of the Breach,
Restorer of Streets with Dwellings."

That tunnel vision—that moment with Paul Cox—was a glimpse of this call. The people lining the walls weren't just part of my imagination. They were my cloud of witnesses, my spiritual lineage. Generations saying Go. Don't be afraid. Let the healing begin.

And it did.

Their voices still echo. You were born for this.
Don't stop now.

Because every time I say yes to healing, to restoration, to telling the truth—I am rebuilding something ancient. I am standing in the breach. I am raising up foundations for others to walk on. I am becoming a place of dwelling. A place where God lives.

A living street, restored.

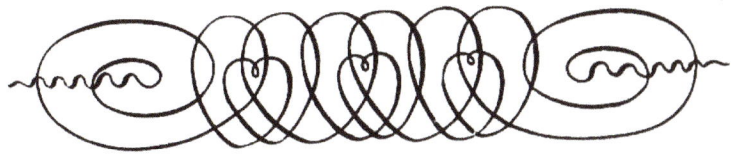

tea
&
revelating

Christine's Prayer

Today and each day as I continue to surrender my entire life to You, the Triune God, I ask for Your Grace to do for me and through me what I cannot do for myself and that You, Holy Spirit, will lead, guide and direct, correct and protect me in all of the paths of Your choosing for my life.

I ask this in that Name above All Names, the One without Whom I cannot live and without Whom I dare not die: Lord Jesus Christ, Son of the Living God.

Christine Potter

"For I know

the plans I have for you."

declares the Lord.

"plans to prosper you

and not to harm you.

plans to give you hope

and a future."

JEREMIAH 29:11

The DREAM becomes REALITY

~ A HOPE ~ A PLAN ~ A FUTURE ~

*H*ave you ever had a dream that didn't make sense at *the time… and then one day, it became your life?*

Years ago, I had a dream where I was living with a woman named Jo. I didn't really know her, but I knew of her. In the dream, I was in her living room, surrounded by high ceilings, a stunning wall of glass with a view that stretched forever, and a towering book wall that I somehow knew hid my room behind it. The space was creative, cozy, and deeply inviting.

But then… a mocking voice. A woman I recognized sat in a chair, questioning my presence there: *"What do you think you're doing here?"* It startled me, but I chose not to give her power. I woke up and tucked the dream away, unsure what it all meant. It never left me.

Some time later, our church was planning a conference. I had every intention of using our own worship teams – until the Lord nudged me: *Invite Jo.* I hesitated, thinking she was surely too busy to invite at the last minute. But I called, and to my surprise, she was available and said yes.

She came. She ministered. And she said something that caught me off guard: *"Let's keep in touch."* I smiled, thinking it was just a polite phrase. I don't do Christianeze well — empty words and good intentions without substance. So, I left it at that.

Sometime later, the Lord asked me to take a sabbatical for June and July. He was calling me back to Himself, to reset and listen. He promised me that by the end of July, I'd know what was next. During that time, I felt the shift. That uncomfortable, being-turned-inside-out kind of shift. The one where everything familiar starts to feel unfamiliar. I knew something was coming — I just didn't know what.

My friend Gail invited me to a conference in Alabama at the end of July. At first, I resisted, wanting to honor my sabbatical. But she was persistent, and eventually, I said yes. Then I found out Jo would be doing worship. I sent her a message about meeting for coffee — and got no reply. I thought, *Well, that's that. Little did I know she had lost her mother right before that time.*

But on the last night of the conference, she was alone on stage, seemingly waiting. I felt prompted to say hello. I walked up — and the moment I did, she said: *"I've been looking for you every night! What are you doing now?"*

I told her I wasn't sure — I felt a shift but had no clarity yet.

*T*hen she said the words that stunned me:

"Would you come live with me and work with me?"
Mind you, I really didn't know her. I was honored, but
I knew God would have to speak.

I was in Shock. The dream flooded back.

This was the dream. I told her I needed to pray about
it, and she understood.

Later, she shared that when she was asking me, she was
just as surprised as I was. She heard herself asking and
thought, *"What am I doing? I don't live with people!"*

But neither of us planned it. God had.

It was His divine setup. A hope. A plan. A future. A dream –
literally – fulfilled. A rite passage fulfilled! He gave me
a preview of things to come… talk about faithful!

That time in my life was so powerful, leading and guiding
me for what was ahead! Just think of a wall of books and
a window that can see forever…

"If anyone
would come after me,
let him deny himself
and take up his cross
and follow me".

MATTHEW 16:24

The DIVINE *S*ETUP:

LETTING GO OF THE KNOWN
TO STEP INTO THE PROMISED

*A*fter leaving that conference, I was stunned – like I had just stepped out of a dream and into a divine setup I didn't see coming.

I knew this wasn't something to process with friends. I needed to hear from God alone. So I asked Him: *"What is this, Lord? What are You asking of me?"*

That's when He brought to mind the parable of the rich young ruler.

"Do you remember him?" He asked.
"Yes," I replied. "He couldn't give up his wealth to follow You."
"Look deeper," He said.

Then it hit me. The rich young ruler hadn't just struggled to give up possessions – he couldn't let go of **who he was**. His identity. His influence. His position. He wasn't just losing things – he was losing *himself* as he knew it.

Then the Lord spoke directly to my heart: *"You've been given a measure of influence and authority. People know you. Can you give all of that back to Me?"*

And there it was. The invitation. The crossroads.

*Y*es, Lord. I'll give it all back to You.

But I had no idea how hard that would be.

Leaving everything – my role, my title, my community, the root system I had – and stepping into a new land where I was unknown, unrecognized, and unrooted, was deeply disorienting. I felt invisible. Lost. Like I had been turned upside down and stripped bare.

I would listen to that worship song on repeat: *"Where You go, I'll go… what You say, I'll say, God…"* Trying to let that become true in my bones.

Back home, I was someone. There's comfort in being known, in having a place. But when God pulls you up by the roots – even to replant you in promise – it hurts.

There were moments I didn't know if I could keep going. I considered giving up. Going back.

But I knew… deep inside… I couldn't. Not if I wanted Him more than I wanted comfort. I was like Abraham, "looking for a city whose architect and builder is God."

So I stayed. I walked it out.

The hardest part wasn't just the move – it was letting go of my identity, in who I was, to receive the identity He was forming in me.

*B*ut now, looking back, I wouldn't trade it.
I learned to trust God's goodness even when the light was dim.
I learned that *He really is enough.*

That alone was worth the price of admission.

That year in Alabama was one of the hardest of my life.
But also one of the most sacred.

He invited me to discover who I really was. I could have
stayed behind and built my ministry, but he asked me to give
it all back to him. In that surrender, He began working it all
together for my good, even though it was painful.

I can't say I was always an overcomer, but I gave all I had.
And apparently, that was enough for Him, and for me.

He walked me through the valley of the shadow of death and
delivered me from a mountain of fear. He knew exactly who
I needed beside me to walk it out.

You see, sometimes people carry the energy and frequency
we haven't yet built in ourselves. That was JoAnn for me,
a true pioneer. Strong. Unafraid. Faithful.

She taught me so much in that season. No wonder God
called her to awaken the prophetic voices of song, He knew
what he was doing then, and He still does.

He led me beside still waters. He restored my soul. He taught me how to be with Him and Him alone.

All of it—the surrender, the pain, the stillness —was preparing me to recognize who He created me to be.

The discovery is still unfolding. Even as I write this, I can see forever just like the window showed me back then.

And the books… well, they're some of the fruit of that journey.

I will forever be grateful —for the dream, the hope, and the plan.

He does a beautiful job weaving the tapestry of our lives… the surrender is so worth it!

ALL
ROADS
LEAD
TO
OBEDIENCE

*When the Lord gives a directive,
he doesn't always give the why with it.
Sometimes, what he asks of us
seems improbable, inconvenient,
or even impossible.*

When the Lord gives a directive, He doesn't always give the why with it. Sometimes, what He asks of us seems improbable, inconvenient, or even impossible. But He kept whispering to me, **"Obedience is better than sacrifice,"** and I knew I needed to pay attention.

This particular ask? A move to Nashville. Completely unexpected. Uninvited. Unfunded. Unexplained.

I tried everything to reason it away. I argued with God: "Lord, surely You're not asking me to go somewhere I haven't been invited. I don't have the money. I don't have a place to stay. What's the point?"

But the gentle voice persisted.

Looking back now, I see how gracious God was to leave signposts along the way—small confirmations that I wasn't imagining things. Even if I didn't understand the why, He was always speaking, always guiding. It reminds me of when Jesus told the disciples they were going through Samaria. They grumbled, confused by the detour. "Why the long way around? Why go where we're not even welcome?" But Jesus had a divine appointment waiting— a woman at a well, a town that would be changed.

He knew what they didn't.

And now, I see: *He knew what I didn't.*

*N*ashville was my Samaria.

The first nudge came after I returned from Israel. I felt a sudden pull toward Nashville but dismissed it. Then, a surprise call from my friend Ruthann—who lives there—rekindled the thought. She said, "Throw your stuff in the car and come on up." So I did. On the drive, another friend texted, "What are you up to?" When I told her, she laughed: "I saw you moving to Nashville yesterday."

Still, I was just visiting friends… or so I thought.

Fast forward to January in Idaho. A woman I didn't know approached me and said, "The Lord told me I've been praying the wrong prayers for you. I was asking Him to bring you here, but He said: *'I have need of her in Nashville.'"* My jaw dropped. It was the third time Nashville had come up, and this time, I couldn't ignore it.

The Lord asked me plainly: **"Will you be obedient, even if you don't understand?"**

And I realized: I didn't need the why. I needed to say yes. He had a plan.

He had already prepared the way in Nashville for me. My friends Steve and Ruthann welcomed me with open arms and prepared a place for me to land. They are some of the finest, most creative people I've ever known. I call them my lifers... It doesn't matter what season of life I'm in, they're always there. I'm so incredibly grateful for their love, wisdom and friendship.

This road led me in a direction I never expected or even dreamed of. That one yes led me to one of the greatest gifts He's ever given me... Carmel! He knew what I needed and what would open up blessings that were unimaginable.

Eye has not seen, or ear has heard nor has it entered into the heart of those who love him, comes to mind... Carmel was that gift... came to life in the most miraculous, beautiful way possible. All because of my YES!

He's such a good Father. He truly is amazing!

But as it is written:

What no eye has seen,
what no ear has heard,
&
what no human mind has conceived~
the things God has prepared
for those who love Him.

1 CORINTHIANS 2:9

Carmel ~
The Journey to the Promise

*I*didn't even remember the promise when it arrived.

Years earlier, while living in Alabama, I heard the Lord whisper to me: *"I'm going to give you a cottage by the sea."* It felt so vivid. So real. And yet, over time, the dream was tucked away, buried under life's transitions and shifting assignments. Until He reminded me again… once I was already standing in it.

The journey to Carmel began with a move from Nashville. My season there had come to a close, and I wasn't sure what was next. Friends made suggestions – including a move back to California – but none felt right. And then, out of the blue, came a mention of a place in Carmel. A couple was looking for someone to serve as a caretaker and intercessor.

My spirit leapt!

Even though they were seeking a couple, I couldn't shake the feeling that this might be for me. Weeks have passed. The door remained closed. I prayed. I waited. I even tried to help find others for the role. Still, Carmel stayed lodged in my heart.

Then came the confirmations.

*F*irst, a friend I had lunch with saw me in the role without knowing I'd already sensed it. Then a phone call with my friend Laura brought everything full circle –Laura said, *"I knew it was you all along,"* she said. *"But you had to hear it from the Lord."*

It was holy ground – that moment of knowing that God had been saving a place for me all along.

When I was interviewed, the Lord said clearly: *Don't discuss money. This is where I'm placing you – trust Me.* I obeyed. The figure I'd originally thought of was far less than what was offered – a reminder that His plans are higher, richer, better than mine.

And when I finally arrived? The cottage sat on the cliffs of Carmel, overlooking the ocean, surrounded by beauty that felt like a dream. And then He spoke again:

"Remember the cottage by the sea I promised you? Well, here you are."

Truthfully, I'd forgotten. He hadn't.

Truthfully, I'd forgotten. He hadn't.

This wasn't just a house. It was a sacred fulfillment –
a love letter written years before, sealed in my spirit, and
delivered in His perfect time. I am still undone by His kind-
ness. It's such a sacred reminder that He has our lives
mapped out if we only agree and believe in His promise and
goodness toward us.

The Cottage

The Gift of Carmel

I thought I'd be there for maybe three years.

That was the plan when I accepted the job in Carmel. Just long enough to help, serve, be useful. But the plan shifted the moment I arrived—and in its place came something bigger: a ten-year assignment, wrapped in beauty, mystery, and a grace I never saw coming.

I didn't know it yet, but Carmel would become one of the greatest gifts of my life.

The property sat on just over three acres, a sanctuary carved into the cliffs above the Pacific. Three dwellings shared the land—each one tucked into the trees and rock as if they'd grown there themselves. From the kitchen window of my cottage, I could see the ocean stretch endlessly to the horizon. My deck overlooked the vastness of creation. It was the kind of place people dreamed of.

D.L. James House

And they said it, over and over, when they came:
"Why didn't you tell me it was this beautiful?"

How could I? How do you describe a place that feels
like Narnia?

I've always loved Carmel. It's a seaside village like no
other–fairytale cottages with thatched roofs, fog rolling in
like a gentle wave, a town steeped in creativity. Clint East-
wood had once been mayor, and the town still hummed with
that quiet, artistic spirit. It was a gathering place for writers,
painters, musicians–seekers of all kinds.

But it wasn't for everyone. Carmel was a hidden gem,
a place mostly the wealthy could afford to call home. I wasn't
wealthy. I was called.

MY ROLE? CARETAKER. INTERCESSOR. CONCIERGE. TRANSLATOR OF THE LAND'S LANGUAGE.

Everything and anything that needed to be done–I did it.
The job was less a title and more a way of life.

I arrived wide-eyed and unprepared. The former caretakers
had just left, and guests were on their way. I knew nothing
about the property. Nothing about the systems or where
anything was kept. Joe, the owner, called and said with a
chuckle, *"Nothing like being thrown into the fire."*

He was right.

But what I didn't expect was how alive the property felt.
It had personality. It spoke. There was something sacred
there–ancient, even. If those walls could talk, I'm sure they'd
have stories worth listening to.

THE LAND HAD A STORY OF ITS OWN.

Known as 'Seaward' and considered a masterwork of architect Charles Sumner Greene, the main house was commissioned in 1918 by D. L. James. Legend said he was related to Jesse James, and while I can't confirm that, I can tell you this: the place had a legacy. James Jr was a writer—some said a screenplay/book writer—and that energy, that creative frequency, still hovered, especially in the greenhouse. Writers who visited often commented on the magic they felt in that space.

When Joe purchased the property, he added the greenhouse and the cottage. The cottage. The one the Lord had whispered to me about long before I ever saw it with my own eyes. And now, there I was—living in it. Breathing in the salt air. Watching the ocean change moods as the tides rolled in and out.

Looking back, it's clear: God was giving me space to heal.

A SACRED PLACE TO BREATHE AGAIN.

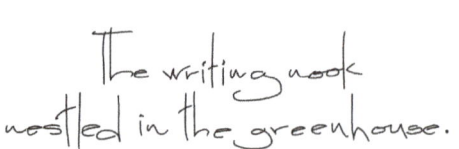

The writing nook nestled in the greenhouse.

Before I ever moved in, I had a dream, and the craziest part was most of that dream literally happened, it was God reassuring me He had it covered and under control.

In the dream, I stood in the kitchen of the main house. Members of the family were there, visibly upset. One of them said, *"We don't want you messing with our inheritance."* I answered, *"I have nothing to do with your inheritance."*

Then Joe appeared. I told him what was happening, and he said, *"That's not going to happen."* He motioned for me to come outside.

The moment we stepped out the door, something shifted. Joe transformed–he became God the Father. He said, *"Come with me."* We rose high above the house, floating over the property. He looked at me and said, *"This is a safe place."*

As He spoke, peace poured over me like warm oil. Then He said something I'll never forget: *"If you need anything at all, remember–my Son lives right downstairs."* What a curious thing to say, but the house was built on a rock and Jesus was the Rock of all ages.

When we returned, the family was leaving. But an old woman, dressed in black mourning clothes, tried to stay behind. She represented sorrow, loss, something ancient and heavy.

I turned to the driver and said, *"No. She cannot stay. She has to go."*

No more mourning. No more death.

That was the moment the staking of the land began.

I don't always know my assignments ahead of time. But the land always reveals itself when I step onto it.

Carmel carried a weight—a sadness, a history that needed healing. I could feel it in the soil, in the trees. The land needed to be loved, appreciated. And I was willing to listen.

I care deeply about beauty. My surroundings matter. Even if things are messy behind the scenes—and they often are—what I see must be beautiful. Carmel gave me that. But it needed care, too.

The trees—some of the most majestic I've ever seen—required tending. The land needed prayer. It took nearly two years to steward it, to spiritually and physically nurture it before it began to change.

But once it did… oh, how it bloomed.

Over time, that land became a place of healing for many.

Joe was one of a kind. Generous, grounded, always caring for people. His wife was just as special. They had a way of making you feel seen, welcomed. It was more than a job—it was a calling. And it was a privilege to serve them for as long as I did.

While there, I learned my calling was as natural as breathing, hospitality was a natural outflow of who He created me to be. I think we can miss those gentle nuances at times.

*S*o many things happened during my years there—stories I'll share another time. But what I know now is this: *Carmel became a safe haven for me.* A sanctuary. A quiet gift from the Lord at just the right time.

I thought I was there to care for the land.
But the land was also caring for me.

I needed that place more than it needed me.
And God knew it all along.

His hand. His mercy. His grace that pursues and overtakes us.

That was the gift of Carmel.

Sanctuary

THE DETOUR!

SAN DIEGO
A DETOUR
A DREAM
A DIVINE ENCOUNTER

was on my way back to Phoenix when our flight got disrupted, they detoured us to San Diego for the night. It disrupted my plans and delayed my return. I wasn't amused at all, I just wanted to get home but San Diego became my landing place for the revelation God was to release.

Do you ever wonder why land is so important to Him? I believe it's the agreement that's on the land with the revelation he's bringing. In this case, He had some things he wanted to show me.

Once there, I got checked into my hotel, and I had a dream. In the dream, I saw a massive angel, his feet planted on the fault line of the southern part of San Diego. He was standing-firm and unshaken, holding the earth together. His assignment was clear; hold it steady until the appointed time. I understood that some Cities are being held by mercy, not merit.

Christine and I were in the house, asleep in bed, resting, when we realized it was time to go to the storehouse.

We entered the place that was full of great abundance. It was overflowing with beautiful fruits and vegetables, colors so bright and vivid that they awakened every sense. The storehouse of heaven was opened! The harvest was not just ripe but it was ready!

We began to prepare, filling brown paper bags with what was needed most. As people began arriving, we seem to know them as they came in and there was more than enough for all.

One woman arrived but paused to use the restroom. We waited. Her bag, filled with provisions, was placed by the door. I knew, this stop was for deliverance. Before she could walk into what was next, she needed to be freed from what was still clinging. We did not rush her as heaven did its quiet work.

Then came the moment that left a mark on me.

 **A**n elderly Native American Chief entered, hand in hand with a young child. They hesitated. Something in him was unsure or perhaps unfamiliar with being received. Possibly because he was bearing the caution of generations. But they entered. And we made their bags ready.

I knew this moment held more than provision. It held prophetic inheritance. The indigenous peoples, the ones who stewarded the land long before walls and borders were once again being welcomed again into the abundance of the Kingdom. The child and the elder walked together, two generations as one, and something powerfully eternal passed between them.

The Clapping of the Trees

After the storehouse, we stepped outside. There were cobblestone paths with shade trees covering the paths and people walking all around. Everything pulsed with such peace. A park ran through the middle of it all.

Then I saw it.

The trees began to sway like a dance with their limbs and leaves clapping. The ground began to rain upwards. There was such a sense of celebration, Creation was rejoicing–not just the beauty that was all around, but with what had just taken place. The sons and daughters of God were receiving what had long been prepared, and Creation was responding!

No one else seemed to notice—but I did. I felt and saw the earth rejoicing with heaven.

I remembered Paul's words:

Creation awaits with eager longing for the revealing of the sons of God ... Creation itself will be set free.

– Romans 8:19-21

I wonder if we can see what the trees see, would we fall to our knees? Would we weep with joy at their profound worship? Their limbs are forever lifted and their roots forever reach. What a picture!

Father, teach us to see and be more like them!

Selah

I'M MY FATHER'S DAUGHTER

I'm my Father's daughter.
I inherit all He has for me.
That is identity, not shame. That is legacy, not limitation

There's a fragrance of remembrance that has begun penetrating our lives. It's wafted its fragrance like a smelling salt to wake us up. We're beginning to see who we truly are and waking up to all the potential inside. We are not only becoming present with ourselves but with each other. The era of shame has long kept us locked up in prisons of our own making. It has been our outerwear, the coat that's protected us! We've worn it well! But… God is breaking through all our barriers so we can be who he has created us to be!!! It's finally here and it's happening.

We're standing at the threshold somewhere between silence and expression, between being hidden and being seen, waking up—not just spiritually, but bodily, and emotionally. We're naming things that were once unspeakable for women because of the shame, and the disconnection from your own well-being and needs. Why have we denied who we are as women? What has been the dialogue in our minds and hearts that has kept us there? If we stop and ask the questions, we become wrecked! He's come to restore all that was taken.

He knows how He made us, and how beautifully intricate we truly are. I think we have forgotten that. I know I have.

Today I'm stripping them of their power over my life.

What are you present to?

We're present to becoming. We're breaking open, but not in a way that's shattering—we're expanding, unfolding. We're no longer content to wear the cloaks of shame, un-worthiness, or "smallness." We're starting to see ourselves as God sees us—whole, worthy, powerful, and chosen.

And that my friend, is Holy Ground!

Sound of her Song

IT'S TIME

Time to give voice to all He has spoken in our lives—
His story through us.

This story—*the making of a king, a priest, and a lover of God*—
could be the subtitle of our lives. It's the *greatest story ever
told*, unfolding through those willing to rise and speak.

After all the centuries of war waged against women—
spiritually, emotionally, physically—it's time to renew what
God started from the beginning. We are reclaiming our land.
Not just in the natural, but in the Spirit. The property of heav-
en—our inheritance—belongs to Him and us. And our **rites of
passage**, long buried or delayed, are being restored.

There is a *chorus rising*, and its sound is holy. The timing is
divine. Truth is stepping into the room again, proclaiming
the **good and acceptable year of the Lord**.

We were made in His image—not to stand behind a man
or ministry, but to stand *alongside* all of humanity. Not in
competition, but in completion.

This is our full inheritance. This is our right. And yes we've
earned it through the fires we've walked and the wars
we've survived.

The days of abuse, silencing, and spiritual takeover—simply because we are women—are coming to an end. We are standing up. We are taking back our ground. Not with weapons of this world, but with the strength of *Kingdom identity*. We stand tall within the borders of God's authority.

In the Kingdom, there is no Jew or Greek, male or female. There is *no separation*. Only union. Only the *image of God* in all its expression.

Now we must show our daughters—*this is their calling too*. They are not sidelined. They are summoned. And so are we.

So take your place. Whatever you're made of—**bring it**. Let the sound of your voice rise.

Because we are here. And we're taking back what's rightfully ours.

PSALM 68:11

THE LORD GAVE THE WORD: GREAT WAS THE COMPANY OF WOMEN WHO PROCLAIMED IT.

The Story That Found Me

Let me begin by saying this: I've never been much of a reader. Growing up, books didn't fill our shelves. Instead, our home was filled with Scripture, hymns, and sermons. We spent nearly all of our time at church — Sunday mornings, Sunday nights, Wednesday night Bible studies, and Friday night services. It was our world, and everything else came second.

We weren't allowed to go to what I now call, sports or entertainment venues. I do remember one special moment, though — a turning point, really. I was 11 when Mary Poppins hit theaters. My neighbor and childhood friend, Cindy Saylors, invited me to go with her family. Going to a movie was against the teachings of our church. In fact, I was told as a child that if Jesus returned and you were in a theater, you'd miss the rapture. But for some reason, my mom said yes — with one caveat: "Don't tell your dad."

"AND WE KNOW THAT IN ALL THINGS GOD WORKS FOR THE GOOD OF THOSE WHO LOVE HIM, WHO HAVE BEEN CALLED ACCORDING TO HIS PURPOSE."

ROMANS 8:28

That movie changed everything. It was magical. It became my "life movie." Looking back now, I can see how Mary's calling to care for and nurture children mirrored what God was preparing in me. I became a mother at 16 – a child with a child – but God took that fragile beginning and turned it into my greatest calling. I've been "Mary" to many, not just my own children. That's the restorative nature of the God we serve: He takes the broken pieces and turns them into beauty.

My father used to say, "You're so heavenly minded, you're no earthly good." I didn't understand it then. But I do now. Even Mary Poppins was a little like that – head in the clouds, heart on a mission.

I often wonder why I never became a reader. Maybe it was because it wasn't modeled at home. Maybe it's because trauma came too early – around 7 or 8 – when my parents began to struggle and my sense of safety was shattered. In many ways, my childhood ended then. And yet, God still stewarded my learning. First came the spiritual – the signs, the wonders, the presence of God in church. That became my education. That became my grounding.

I may not have learned through pages, but I learned by watching. I'm an observer. I read rooms more than I read books.

If anything in my life speaks, I pray it's this: that Christ is at the center. That He is faithful. That He redeems, rebuilds, and restores what was broken. This is my legacy – the most precious gift I can give my family. A life lived with eyes on heaven and hands open to serve.

And here's the sweetest irony of all: for a girl who never read much, my life now is a story – The Book of Bonita, Habakkuk 2 says…write your vision/story, make it plain so all that pass by my read and know!

Letting Go

a mothers heart

Train up a child in the way he should go;
even when he is old he will not depart from it.
– Proverbs 22:6

How do we not become a mom?

It's funny to even ask that question, because if there's one role I've lived and loved deeply–it's being a mother. I love my family with everything in me. If you asked my daughter, she'd probably say, "Yes, a little too much." She's taught me so much–wise beyond her years, a tower of strength and courage. For context, she's 54, not 14, though I confess, sometimes I forget that.

She'll gently (or not-so-gently) remind me: *"Mom, I'm not a baby."* And she's right.

$\mathcal{B}$ut the only way I've ever known how to love… is like a mom. That fierce, all-in kind of love that wants to protect, correct, guide, and nurture. And honestly, **letting go of that role—of who I've been to them—is hard.**

I still see them as my kids, even when they're grown. I still want to offer advice, give direction, and pour out affection. That part of me doesn't shut off. I don't think it ever will. But I'm learning to let go with grace—to trust that I've done the best I could, even with all the bumps and missteps in between.

Because here's what I know now: there's no perfect family. We all have our "stuff." But love, when it's real, finds its way through.

My sons joke with me, motioning with their hands: *"Mom, you're way up here. and I need you here."*

Sons. They say it with love, but the truth is, they're grown too. Capable. Strong. Becoming the men God designed them to be. And they don't need me in the same way anymore.

That's the real release: not letting go of them, but letting go of who I once was to them. Making space for a different kind of relationship—one rooted in respect, mutual love, and trust. One where I sit back and watch the fruit of my labor blossom in their lives. One where I'm asked in, not always needed.

Relationships can be hard. But they're also beautiful.

I want to grow into that place of wisdom that knows when to speak and what to speak. That's the next layer of letting go. The gentle kind. The sacred kind. The kind that doesn't demand space but is always ready when invited in.

Because the truth is, I'll always be a mom. But now, I'm learning to be a **wise one**.

Wisdom is calling...

GOD in the GOOSE CHASES

He will cover you with His feathers, and under His wings you will find refuge; His faithfulness will be your shield and rampart.— Psalm 91:4

When I think back on vacations, it's surprising how few I can clearly recall. We didn't take many, and when we did, they were often simple road trips around California – the beach, Disneyland. Nothing extravagant. But still, a few moments shine through the fog of memory, like a sunbeam through clouds.

One of those memories takes me to Oregon. My dad, my sister, and I visited my Aunt Ann – the only girl among four brothers. She was bold, feisty, and knew who she was. I adored her. That trip left an impression, not because of what we did, but because of how I felt. Known. Loved.

Maybe even a little bit like her.

THEN THERE WAS THE GOOSE.

Yes— one stubborn, angry goose in a park who decided to chase toddler-me in circles while my dad stood nearby laughing so hard he could barely breathe. I cried. He laughed. And my Aunt Ann scolded him for it. To this day, I'm still not a fan of geese. But somehow, I can laugh about it now, too. Life has a way of turning even the strangest stories into treasures.

Another vacation that marked me was to Arizona, visiting my parents' dear friends, Ruth and Orland. Ruth had prayed over me before I was born – a spiritual midwife of sorts. On the way home from that trip, my father bought me a Native American ring and bracelet at a roadside shop. They weren't extravagant gifts, but I treasured them.
My father, part Cherokee, saw something special in that moment. And so did I. It was one of those rare times he did something out of the ordinary just for me, and it has stayed with me my whole life.

These few memories – a goose, a bullfight, a ring in the desert – seem disconnected at first. But looking closer, I can see how God was present in all of them. In the laughter, in the fear, in the love expressed through small gifts. Even in the chaos, there was a thread of grace weaving it all together.

Vacations were rare, but they weren't without meaning. And maybe that's the lesson – that even when life doesn't look like everyone else's, even when our childhoods were more about church pews than sandy beaches, God was still writing a story. A rich one. A sacred one. One where even wild goose chases become part of the testimony.

Life has a way of turning even the strangest stories into treasures.

The Tree of Lights

Ayden

The learning tree is life to me
It Illuminates my mind you see

Sitting beneath it shines with care
To help me see what's really there

Imaginations at its best
Dancing like light upon my head
Free from all fear and dread

From young to old – Come one come all
From inside you'll grow so very tall

Dreamers are safe and free to be
Engaging with heaven's marvelous tree

Come sit beneath this marvelous light
Come see what makes it shine so bright

Sent from heaven above to display its worth
This tree, this life this sacred birth

'Twas in the garden long before
This tree of life holds so much more

Books unread From ages past
and those to come that lie ahead

This tree of life and its life giving flow
With waters found from deep below

From ages past to futures before
It always shows the open door

Come sit beneath its light you'll see
Heavens one and only beautiful tree

Do I Dare Write This?

Do I dare write about this…

Have you ever had those days where loneliness wraps around you like a heavy blanket? I have. The raw truth of feeling lost and alone, disconnected from everyone. Yes—even in marriage, we can feel terribly alone.

Because real connection isn't just proximity—it's heart communication. And without it, we lose touch.

But our most important connection? It's with God Himself.

And here's the thing: sometimes I run from Him. I hide—like Adam and Eve in the garden. Even though He already knows what's in my heart before I speak it, I still find myself avoiding eye contact with Heaven.

Why?

Maybe I don't want to be fully seen. Maybe I'm afraid to enter into his hope. When our desired outcomes are delayed or postponed, it can lead us into despair. But the truth is—He's closest when I'm walking through despair. That's when I need to run toward Him, not away.

Hope deferred makes the heart sick. but when the desire comes. it's the tree of life. Proverbs 13:12

Could it be that these patterns—this isolation—are just boxes we've built in our hearts?

Safe, quiet places where we believe we're protected... but we're actually imprisoned.

I've been good at isolating. Too good. God has been faithful to walk me out of my times of isolation… I'm becoming more secure in His love, I'm beginning to see the triggers. To name them. To no longer be so easily overtaken by them. And that, right there, is the beginning of overcoming.

For in Him we live and move and have our being. Even as our own poets have said. we are His offspring. Acts 17:28

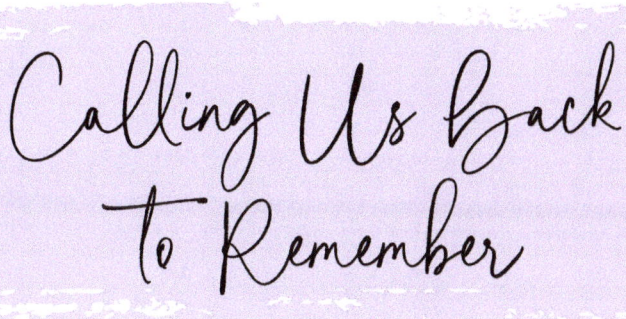

Calling Us Back to Remember

He's always calling us back –
not to punish, not to shame –
but to **re-member** us.
To put us back together again.
To restore what we've forgotten:
who we are, and who we are in Him.

He's always molding, equipping, and teaching us about
the one He created us to be. It's so easy to get swept up
in the current of life and leave Him in the background.
But He never moves. He never stops speaking.
He never stops loving.

Through every moment
– the messy, the mundane, and the miraculous –
He's there.

Sometimes I find myself praying,
**"Take me back… back to that place where I was in You,
and You were in me… before time began."**

He took me somewhere in the Spirit.
I was taken to this place. inside of Him
~ we literally were one.
I don't just believe it – I remember it.

That place of complete union, of being, Echad.
Oneness. Where there was no separation.
I saw and felt so clearly who he is, His power,
His presence, the overwhelming peace that
covered the earth and the heavens. I realized
then that all my worries were for nothing.
He is the I Am, the shalom,
the wholeness of everything.
Words don't adequately describe it.
But He leaves us with an open invitation
into the knowing of who He is.
I was in Him – inside the Vine.
And He was in me.

It wasn't just peace –
it was the fullness of wholeness.
Nothing missing.
Nothing broken.
His governance.
His compassion.
His creativity.
His tenderness.
I could feel His gaze over His creation –
and He loved what He saw.
He wasn't disturbed.
He wasn't anxious.
He was **love**, through and through.

And in that space, I was there – part of it.
The most holy encounter I've ever had.

The memory of it remains etched
in the deepest places in me.

It's more than memory — it's truth.

Can you imagine? The God of the universe…
carries us – all of us – in His heart.

We've just forgotten.

But when we remember **Him**,
we start to remember **ourselves**.

Because there is no separation.
Not really.
Not ever.
He is here.
Now.
Always.

He was there at the beginning.
He'll be there at the end.
And He's never stopped calling us back
– not to a doctrine, but to **union**.
To the original oneness we shared with Him
before the foundations of the world.

And in that remembering, we are re-membered.
Made whole again.

Hearing the TRUTH

You Don't Want to Hear

Throughout the years of my life, I've discovered a truth:

THERE ARE THINGS I'D JUST RATHER NOT HEAR.

You see, I was raised in Pentecost—a world of rules and legalism. A long list of don'ts, so to speak. For example: if you went to the movies and Jesus came back, you wouldn't go with Him. The same went for football games, playing cards—basically most things fun. It was always about *where* you were and *what* you were doing when Jesus returned. God was portrayed more like an angry monitor than a loving Father. Fear and control were the primary motivators—keeping the "saved" ones saved through constant dread. I grew up feeling more like a disappointment to God than someone deeply loved by Him.

It's taken me years to unlearn that fear-based religion. And honestly, it still tries to rear its head now and then. But I've walked through what I call the "school of love" with my Father. He's been gently removing the echoes of fear from the very cells of my being. Because fear leaves a mark. When we serve out of fear, we can't fully know or understand the love of God.

It's been a long healing journey—and I'm still on it.

That's why, for years, I avoided anything to do with end-time teaching. It triggered that childhood fear, and I pushed it away, convinced that the whole message had been misinterpreted.

I believed God wasn't about religion or dogma—just love. It was easier to think we were already in the time frame where things were only going to get better.

Then, something shifted.

At the beginning of this year, I suddenly found myself surrounded by Hebraic tribes, which I love, but it took me by surprise. I kept asking, *God, what is this? I thought we were settled with the end time message?*

But He was so patient. He let me wrestle. He didn't scold me for my doubt. Instead, He kept asking, *Do you trust Me? Do you believe I love you? Can we let go of this fear together?*

He wasn't out to punish me. He wasn't looking to hurt me. He was inviting me—again—into healing.

It didn't fit the narrative I had in my heart. But I've learned that when something new shows up as a trigger, it might just be time for another layer of healing.

So I kept watching. Listening.

And the more I did, the more things started to line up. There was *truth* there—not that I understood it all, but something in my spirit recognized it. I was no longer fixated on fear.

Yana and Darla played a big part in that. These women walk with honesty, vulnerability, and no pretense. This walk has been very costly for them both. The "One New Man" message—encapsulated in their lives—isn't driven by the old religious machine. It's not polished, popular, or platform-driven. And because of that, it's been misunderstood, even attacked. But it's real.

I may not understand everything, but I know this: God is showing me truth. He's still meeting me in the places where fear was the voice. And He's loving me through the transformation.

I don't follow Him out of fear. I honor Him with my life because I love Him—and I don't want to hurt the One who loves me so deeply. I no longer see Him as a harsh judge with a gavel in hand, but as the patient, merciful, and loving Father that He is.

Where He's leading, I don't fully know. But I do know this— there's been a massive shift.

I'm trusting Him to lead.

He's got me.
He's got my family.
He's got those I love.

For perfect LOVE casts out all fear.

You have my **Yes**

WHEN THE LION OVERTAKES YOU

Have you ever had an experience you simply couldn't explain? I have.

It happened one day during a conference. I was on stage with the worship leader himself–Steve–and I could feel the atmosphere begin to shift. I'm a feeler, and I knew something was about to break open in the spirit. Intercession was getting ready to land.

While worship continued, one of the speakers came over to me and whispered in my ear, *"You have something."* I responded honestly, *"I don't have any words right now."* But again, she insisted, *"You have something."*

I was trembling. I didn't know which way to go–there were no words, only a stirring. So I stayed seated. She stood right beside me. And one more time, she said it: *"You have something."*

And that's when it happened.

I stepped down off the stool and in doing so the Lion of Judah overtook me. It was as if I was inside of Him–literally *inside*. I could hear His breathing. With every shake of His mane, I felt it pulse through my body. He began to prowl around the stage–moving here and there with a strength and purpose that wasn't my own.

I was along for the ride.

My ears were tuned to His voice. The sounds He made were from a heavenly realm–growls, groans, deep rumblings of war. I realized He was moving toward the podium where the speaker was ministering. What a sight it must have been for the congregation.

And all the while… my mother was in the audience.

I remember thinking, *Why today? What will she think?*
But I was too far gone to care. I was inside the Lion—hearing
His sound, sensing His intention.

He was on the move. And whatever had stirred Him to rise
that day, He was dealing with it.

That encounter has marked me forever. Even now, when
I recall it, I can hear Him. His breath. His voice.

Why am I sharing this story?

Because I believe when we say **yes**, He invites us into
adventures with Him. He never forces—He invites.

That day, I had the choice to shut it all down. I could have
let fear of what others might think keep me seated. But I
didn't. And I'm so glad I didn't.

I truly encountered the **Lion of the Tribe of Judah**.
His breath.
His sound.
His movement.
His warfare.
He was on the move—and I got to move with Him.

We are entering a time where we will need the supernat-
ural more than ever. This book—this collection of stories—
is meant to encourage you.

Take the risk. Don't let fear stand in your way. Say yes, even
when it's wild. Even when you have no grid for what He's
doing.

All He's looking for is your **yes**. And when you give it,
He'll take you places you never imagined.

Yes!

FREE FALL

As for me and my house, we will serve the Lord.
Joshua 24:15

Letting go isn't giving up—it's making space for what really counts.

If there's a recurring theme in my life—and in nearly everything I write—it's this: LETTING GO.

Over and over, God invites me into the same sacred posture: open hands, surrendered heart. In my spirit, I call it the **free fall**—the beautifully terrifying, exhilarating moment when I release control and lean into His arms.

Letting go doesn't come naturally. It rubs against everything in our humanity that craves certainty, safety, and stability. But when we become even a little aware of His **immeasurable love**, we begin to trust. We begin to loosen our grip—not just on things, but on fears, expectations, and even identities we've outgrown.

Because most of the time, it's fear that holds us back. And fear—if we're honest—signals **lack**. But the Kingdom of God is built on **abundance**. On fullness. On more than enough.

So, when He asks us to let go—of our thoughts, our emotions, our anger, our livelihoods, our relationships—it's not punishment. It's invitation.

An invitation to freedom.

An invitation to clarity.

An invitation to make **space for what really counts**.

Those words echo in my soul like a psalm:

"Letting go isn't giving up — it's making space for what really counts."

Selah. Think about these things.

When God calls us into a new season, He doesn't always tell us what's next. But He asks for our trust—because **He knows the beginning from the end**. He is Alpha and Omega. And He doesn't waste a single thing we surrender.

So if you find yourself in that sacred space of release, that free fall of faith—remember this: He's not asking you to give up. He's asking you to make room.

Because what's coming… matters more than what you've had to let go.

If these Walls could Speak

The truth is, I've been a wreck at times. Carmel became my detox—a holy pause I didn't know I needed. I hadn't realized how tired I truly was until I got there. Slowly, like pieces of a puzzle turning right side up, the layers of exhaustion, grief, and ministry began to surface.

Before Carmel, I had lived most like a missionary—going wherever the Lord sent me, on prayer assignments that stretched across seasons and states. He was always faithful to bring me back to life in those times. The faith walk can be exhilarating, yes, but it can also be lonely, bewildering, and costly. And yet, I had been loved well along the way.

I had been welcomed into homes and ministries, sat at tables of spiritual richness, and shared life with some of the finest people I've ever known. Sometimes I was a little broken, but I was carried, too.

Leaving Arizona—my safe nest after my divorce—was not easy. People like Cory and Kena were the first to step in when I had nothing left. Their lives radiate healing to anyone who enters their realm. They offered me safety and unconditional love when I needed it most. I will always be grateful for that chapter.

And there are so many others—too many to name—whose light carried me. I am forever grateful for every one of them.

Then came the Potters.

Oh, what a gift. I knew it from the very first meal—when we shared dessert from the same plate. Something in me just knew: These are my people. They took me in as one of their own and began to teach me the ways of the Kingdom. Gently. Patiently. They loved me back to life. I was so green and so fearful, but they never rushed me. They taught me how to stand. They were my answer when God asked me, "What do you want?" And when He whispered, "Done," I believed Him.

And then came JoAnn.

Sister Hair entered my life like no one else could. She introduced me to the edge—to those who leap with God into the unknown. Jo is one of the most fearless people I know. Watching her challenged every fear I still held. She was a pioneer, forging paths for others and championing people into their purpose. We had our ups and downs, sure—but our friendship endured, and the Lord wove our stories together with a fierce kind of grace. To this day, I am proud to call her my good friend.

Isn't it something how God weaves our lives like tapestries? Thread by thread, person by person, what once seemed random becomes holy. And somehow, when we let go, it all becomes beautiful.

I can't forget my Alabama tribe—Steven and Stacey Shelley. It started at a Chinese restaurant. God had a plan in that meeting. Looking back now, I can see His orchestration so clearly. They didn't just welcome me—they remodeled a home for me. They made it beautiful. They made it safe. I was only there for a season, but it left a permanent mark. I didn't always fit the mold, and I probably scared the stuffing out of half the congregation, but they loved me anyway. That's family. That's Kingdom.

I had dreams about Alabama, and every one of them was fulfilled. Life in Christ is so rich, so full of joy. We just have to remember the journey. And in remembering the journey, we remember ourselves—and the life we have in Him.

Then came Nashville, my "road to Samaria"

—an out-of-the-way place to meet who the Lord had next. God knows how to weave the tapestry together with who he calls for those seasons. He brings people together, whether it's in Chinese restaurants or on the road to Samaria… lives are changed and recorded within those journeys. Thank you Ruthann and Steve, Larry and Laura, Nancy and Rick for being so amazing on that road to Nashville. My time there was so beautiful!

And then came Carmel.

Carmel held beauty.

Carmel held treasure.

Carmel held rest for the weary.

What a gift it was. Truly, a healing time.

If these walls could speak, they would tell stories of dreams and black Cadillacs, of laughter and trembling prayers, of the best of the best who walked me through fire and into light. They would tell of a woman who came undone… so she could be re-membered. The promises are still unfolding, and prayers yet to be answered, from our Heavenly Father who delights in restoring what once was broken. and if you listened closely beneath the sound of the ocean and in the quiet moments, you'd hear it still: the sound of becoming.

*I am a woman refashioned.
bearing the image of my Father.*

She Will Arise

she will arise from these ashes.

she will survive her trespasses.

She will arise to tell her story.

She will arise in all her glory.

She will arise~

She will arise

Author

Bonita Blakeman is a writer and spiritual storyteller whose journey of faith has led her down roads less traveled—pathways marked by both brokenness and beauty, all leading toward transformation.

Her life tells a raw yet redemptive story of learning to walk with God through unexpected encounters, weaving together moments of breakdown and breakthrough on the way to healing.

After years of serving in ministry as a worship pastor, missionary, and intercessor, she laid it all down to follow Him more deeply. In the process, she discovered her true identity in the One who created her, and learned that life in Yeshua is far more than she ever imagined possible.

She makes her home in Arizona, where the lights of her life are her family—her children, grandchildren, and great-grands—along with her beloved tribe of friends. Bonita's passions flow from creativity and from helping others discover their own unique sound—their voice—writing to awaken the hidden treasures within us all. Through her words, she hopes readers will encounter the beauty of God's healing presence in their own stories.

https://bonitablakeman.com/

Illustrations

Illustrations by Ruthann Fryer unless otherwise noted. Graphics drawn by Ruthann or sourced from out-of-date books, catalogues, etc.

Credit to the following artists:

Pg. 49   *'Girl with Lipstick'*
          - Ruthann's painting after
          Norman Rockwell 1894-1978
          American Magazine cover 1922

Pg. 54   *'The Sower'* 1888
          - Vincent Van Gogh 1853-1890

Pg. 70   *'Book of Bonita'* collage
          - Bonita Blakeman

Pg. 88   *California Landscape*
          - Percy Gray 1869-1952

Pg. 120 *'Tree of Lights'* 2025
          - Ayden Barrett

Pg. 122   - Unidentified artist -1800's

Photographs:
Bonita Blakeman's personal collection

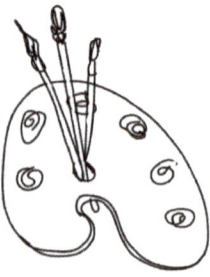

 **Ruthann Fryer** is a thoughtful and creative individual who carries both a quiet presence and a bold confidence in Christ. As an artist with a poetic sensibility, she is deeply passionate about pursuing truth, cultivating peace, and being shaped by love. Her life reflects a continuous journey of spiritual depth, marked by a surrendered heart and a growing awareness of joy as her daily portion.

Her path has often been one of hiddenness – deeply rooted in a life centered in Christ.

In addition to her creative work, Ruthann is a caring wife, mother, and grandmother. She has a deep appreciation for family heritage and finds joy in sharing stories that testify to the enduring goodness of God.

Together with her husband, Steve – a musician/artist and fellow creative – they live in – and work on – their historic 1800's log farmhouse and studio, nestled in the rolling hills of Tennessee. Their surroundings offer a place for reflection and inspiration.

"My work flows from a life rooted in stillness, wonder, and the presence of Christ. As an artist and poet, I create from a contemplative space – where brushstrokes and words become both expression and encounter. I work in several mediums, but oil painting and poetic writing hold a special place in my heart. I find joy in the fullness of expression with a touch of whimsy."

TESTIMONIALS

Bonita's authenticity of expression brings not only treasures from God's heart to yours but stirs remembrance of your own interactions with Him through the years. Her book carries an 'anointing of remembrance', something I've not come across before, resulting in faith, hope and intimacy renewed. As she is my closest of friends, I can honestly say she speaks with purity of heart to bring us closer to 'the One our hearts doth love...whom we will not let go.' - Song of Songs 3:4

– JoAnn McFatter

I found out that the word "witness" means evidence. This delightful book is evidence of God's amazing faithfulness. The title could just be "Letting Go" among a number of others. Though it is full of reallife situations that many of us face, it is also full of some very painful things that only God could orchestrate and deliver her through. All the time I've known Bonita, I never picked up a hardened heart from the pain she has endured, or an overly religious person after being touched by God. Though my wife and I are fondly mentioned in this book, (and I am a bit prejudiced,) I feel it's important to point out the antidotes she offers to counteract the poison that life sometimes deals us. These are made clear in these few pages at the cost of full exposure. Good job Bonita, I love it.

– Don Potter

Family. Table. Feast. Laughter. Remembrance.

Words can paint a picture. Words can create a feast for the reader - as morsels of truth bring life. And words can become a lighted pathway that beckons the reader to journey inward as well as forward. This book exemplifies each one.

Bonita, dear friend, this book is a bountiful feast spread before us as you serve your life, and it's quite a harvest! It is joyful. It is sacred and precious. How glorious it is to 'fellowship one with another' in His light.

– Ruthann Fryer

Heaven's Heart for Earth

Seraph Creative is a collective of artists, writers, theologians & illustrators who desire to see the body of Christ grow into full maturity, walking in their inheritance as Sons of God on the Earth.

Sign up to our newsletter to know about future exciting releases.

Visit our website: www.seraphcreative.org

www.ingramcontent.com/pod-product-compliance
Lightning Source LLC
Chambersburg PA
CBHW051203120626
46547CB00012B/1178